Xenophobe's®
guide to the
ITALIANS

Martin Solly

Xenophobe's Guides

Published by Xenophobe's® Guides.
E-mail: info@xenophobes.com
Web site: www.xenophobes.com

Printed 2019

Editor – Catriona Tulloch Scott
Series Editor – Anne Tauté
Cover designer – Vicki Towers
Map – Jim Wire
Printer – CPI Antony Rowe, Wiltshire

Illustrations – Gunda Urban & Franziska
Feldmann, courtesy of the German edition
of this book, *So sind sie, die Italiene,*
published by Reise Know How Verlag.

Additional illustration – Colosseum ©Arya
Falanesca from Shutterstock.

Cover: Gondolier awaiting tourists in Venice, Italy
©arenaphotouk; Ferrari ©Francesco Dazzi/
Shutterstock.com

Grateful thanks are given to Federica Caratelli,
Michelangelo Conoscenti, and especially
Federico Tibone for their help and information.

ePub ISBN: 9781908120601
Mobi ISBN: 9781908120618
Print ISBN: 9781906042394

Contents

The Italian population is 62 million – compared with
8 million Swiss, 8 million Austrians, 10 million Greeks,
56 million English, 66 million French, 81 million Germans,
and 325 million Americans.

Italy is 7 times larger than Denmark and 3 times larger than
Austria, but could fit nearly twice into France.

Nationalism & Identity

Nations within a nation

The Italians are not a race, but a collection of peoples. They tend to think of themselves and each other first and foremost as Romans, Milanese, Sicilians or Florentines, and second as Italians. There is little that really links Turin and Bari, or Naples and Trieste, except the autostrada, the high speed rail network and the Catholic Church.

> **Deeply ingrained regionalism is quite understandable considering that Italy has only existed as a nation since 1861.**

The regions of Italy are very different from one another and the deeply ingrained regionalism is quite understandable considering that Italy has only existed as a nation since 1861, before which the Italian peninsula consisted of several independent states. The unification process required a skilful exercise in geopolitical patchwork, and the leading politicians of the time were well aware of the difficulties facing them. They included Massimo D'Azeglio who said: 'Italy has been made at last; now let us make the Italians.' Were he alive today, he would still be working at it.

Every now and then the Italians do try and behave like a nation and make a big effort to be nationalistic, for example, when the Italian football team is doing well in the World Cup, or Ferrari has just won the

1

Formula One World Championship twice in a row. But mostly the Italians feel like Italians when they are expatriates: in an ice-cream parlour in Melbourne, down a Belgian mineshaft, or at a soccer match in the United States.

In reality it scarcely matters since all Italians know that, of course, they do everything 'better'. They may not generally display their strong belief in themselves and their nation, but when it does surface it can be most impressive. In 2011 the country marked its 150th birthday party with a dignified yet joyous celebration of national identity. In towns and villages throughout the country, red, white and green flags were hung from virtually every balcony in an effervescent display of pride at being Italian, showing that the country has come a long way since it was described by Metternich, the 19th-century Austrian statesman, as a 'mere geographical expression'.

> **66 Mostly Italians feel like Italians when they are expatriates. 99**

The national anthem, however, is a different matter. When it was noticed in a TV close-up before a football international that none of the Italian team (the jewel in the nation's crown) was actually singing Italy's anthem, it was realised that not only did they not know the words but few other Italians knew them either. The media have remedied the situation by playing the anthem more and, whenever possible, with subtitles.

The absence of overtly nationalistic feelings makes

Italians wary of warmongering and jingoism. Knowing that most disputes can be resolved by a mixture of compromise, appeasement and bribes, they will do their best to avoid confrontation. In fact, any foreign power planning to invade Italy should consider making an offer for it before wasting soldiers' lives. If the price is right, it is quite conceivable that the Italians might agree to sell their country.

Campanilismo

Identity is important to the Italians and they are particularly attached to their roots. 'Where do you come from?' is an important question for them which requires a good answer. Unlike an Englishman or American, no Italian is at a loss when asked this question. He does not mutter, 'I'm not really sure. Let me think. I was born in Hertfordshire, but my parents moved to Leeds, and I went to university in Bristol and then my first job was in York…'

Italians know exactly where they come from and will carry that place around with them for ever, like a standard. The man from San Giorgio in Puglia who lives in Turin will maintain his links with San Giorgio all through his life. Even if he left the town 30 years ago, and only goes back once a year to see his second cousins, he will

> 66 Italians know exactly where they come from and will carry that place around with them for life, like a standard. 99

3

still have to help anyone else who comes from San Giorgio. Similarly, successful tycoons and politicians are expected to look after their hometowns, investing money in them and finding work for their fellow towns-folk.

> **❝ Italians know that other Italians are sadly lacking in self-discipline and cannot be trusted. ❞**

Stating where you come from is closely linked to the key Italian concept of *campanilismo*, which literally means 'loyalty to your local bell-tower', but really involves thinking that your village or town is the best in the world. Italians have always loved their hometowns and found it hard to be exiled from them.

Such civic pride also implies competitiveness, and this is especially strong between neighbouring villages, towns, provinces and regions. The rivalry is often so fierce that Italians have little time left for much else, for they know that other human beings, especially Italians from other families, villages, towns or regions, have to be watched. They are sadly lacking in self-discipline and cannot be trusted. How wonderful Italy would be without *gli altri* – 'those other' Italians.

How others see them

The typical stereotype of the Italians is of a noisy, passionate, scheming, Mediterranean people, whose brilliance and inventiveness are unfortunately marred by laziness and unreliability.

With unwitting masochism, Italians genuinely rather enjoy seeing their faults highlighted. It confirms their own deep-rooted feeling that *gli altri Italiani* are not quite up to the western world's high standards of dependability. But no criticism is ever taken seriously enough to attempt remedial action.

In any case, foreigners seem to find the locals agreeable and entertaining, so it cannot be all bad.

It is universally acknowledged that Italians live in a beautiful country full of art treasures. They are seen as a happy, fun-loving people, with a genius for design, food and fashion. They are known to be wonderful at singing and at cooking, and terrible at organising. Italian men are supposed to be dark, handsome and demon lovers; Italian women to be sultry and attractive, wonderful cooks and doting mammas.

Italo-Americans often imagine that Italy hasn't changed since their great-grandparents left it at the turn of the last century. When they finally come to Italy to find their roots and visit their cousins, they are surprised that not all families are poor, have ten children and live in one room which they share with a donkey and a mongrel; that not all the women wear

5

black and work in the fields, nor do all the men wear hats and sit in bars all day long. They discover that Italy is, in fact, one of the world's most advanced countries, where most families have at least two cars and live in houses that don't just have running water and electricity, but plasma screen televisions, broadband Internet access, high tech cellphones and bidets with mixer taps and adjustable jets.

How they see themselves

The Italians see themselves as passionate, intelligent, humorous and charming and they like to act the part for the benefit of foreigners.

They know they are privileged living in the most beautiful country in the world. In fact, apart from wishing they could contract out the running of their country to Brussels, all would be paradise... if they didn't have those nagging doubts about their fellow citizens.

Special relationships

Because of the massive emigration from Italy at the end of the 19th and beginning of the 20th centuries, there are extensive Italian communities in the United States, Argentina, Brazil, Uruguay and Australia. There are about 20 million Americans with Italian surnames. But Italo-Americans, Italo-Argentinians and so on are only likely to be regarded in the mother country as 'Italians', rather than as Americans or Argentinians, if they are rich and successful. So Rudolph Giuliani, Frank Sinatra, Robert De Niro, Francis Ford Coppola and Sylvester Stallone are all considered to be Italian, and not American. Some famous Italians, who changed their names to achieve success in the New World, such as actress Anne Bancroft, born Anna Maria Italiano in New York in 1931, and crime novelist Ed McBain, born Salvatore Lombino in 1926 also in New York, have only been welcomed back into the fold on their decease.

66 There are about 20 million Americans with Italian surnames. 99

Being embraced so warmly can sometimes have its drawbacks – successful paternity suits were still being brought in the Naples courts against the Italo-Argentinian, Diego Maradona, years after he returned home to Argentina.

How they see foreigners

Italians love foreigners, especially rich foreigners. The Austrians, Swiss and Germans have always enjoyed Italy's climate, culture, beaches and lifestyle. Italy is their playground. Ever since the days of the Roman Empire, Goths have been heading across the Alps to let off steam. The Italians have tolerated them for centuries and are quite happy to go on doing so, as long as the six million who now come to Italy every year spend lots of money and return home again.

The French are considered arrogant and disproportionately proud of themselves. They are seen to look down on their transalpine neighbours, which peeves the Italians no end. But the really unforgivable French sin is to have captured the world market with their inferior wine, which no sane Italian would buy.

The relationship between the English and the Italians is more complex and perhaps more an attraction of opposites. The English like the violent smells, noises, colours, passions and chaos of Italy, while the Italians are intrigued by the order and cosiness of the English, but pity them for their rainy weather, dull food and general lack of style.

> **❝ Italians feel sure that everything works much better abroad. But they are also sure that foreigners are less well-off because they don't live in Italy. ❞**

Italians feel sure that everything works much better abroad. But they are also sure that, in real terms, foreigners are less well-off than they are because they don't live in Italy with its plentiful sunshine, they dress badly, and they eat and drink badly, all of which perhaps explains why foreigners have always had their eye on Italy.

Being a curious people, the Italians are fascinated by foreigners and their barbaric ways of life. They love reading and hearing about other countries and going abroad on holiday as this serves to confirm what they already know, that they come from the best place in the world, certainly in terms of the important things in life like sunshine, drink, food and football. Deep down, the Italians believe the sentiments nicely captured by their proverb: '*Tutto il mondo è paese*' (it's the same the whole world over): that although other nations might be more powerful and better organised than their own, in reality the rest of the world behaves the same way they do and is just as corrupt as they are, only sometimes the others are smarter at not being caught.

How they see immigrants

Large scale foreign immigration is a comparatively recent phenomenon in Italy. Traditionally, the word 'immigrant' was used by Italians for Italians from other parts of Italy who had moved to their area. But more and more people have arrived to make their homes in Italy, mainly from Albania, Eastern Europe, Senegal, Nigeria, Latin America, Asia and the Maghreb countries. Official records show that the proportion of foreign-born residents in Italy increased from under 1% in 1990 to over 7% in 2010, a huge change for a country which had previously been famous for its emigration.

The Italian attitude towards the peoples of Eastern

Europe and northern Africa is a mixture of solidarity and disdain. They like their colour and are fascinated by their strange habits, and they especially like the fact that the immigrants do work that they might otherwise have to do. They agree with the sentiment expressed in the Oscar-winning Italian film *Mediterraneo,* that all the people around this sea compose *una faccia, una razza* (one face, one race). Yet they resist being associated with poor immigrants, like the Albanians or North Africans who offer to clean their car windows at traffic lights, for fear that their glamorous image might get tarnished. There have been a few incidences of racial discrimination, but Italians are generally more tolerant of foreigners than of other Italians.

> **Many Italian factory owners know that they would probably have to close down without the immigrants.**

A large number of immigrant families manage to find seasonal jobs in the countryside, picking tomatoes and grapes, while others settle in the industrial cities in the north of the country where they do the manual work that no longer attracts young Italians. Many Italian factory owners know that they would probably have to close down without the immigrants. These days most home helps and old age carers in Italy are foreigners, and some of the immigrant communities have achieved surprising economic success, starting up small businesses even in occupations where the locals have traditionally ruled the roost: there are now Egyptian owned and run pizzerias and Chinese leather factories.

The immigrants are responsible for the rise in Italy's population, which until recently had been declining due to the fall in the indigenous population's birthrate. This has led to a curious dichotomy: the immigrants are seen by some as a threat to the Italianness and Italian values of the nation, yet without their hard work those values might disappear. After all it is only the taxes and pension contributions paid by the 'new Italians' that enable the country's increasingly numerous pensioners to enjoy their retirement.

North and South

The Italians simplify their internal differences by means of a straightforward North–South divide.

The Northern Italian views the Southern Italian as a corrupt, half-Arab peasant who tolerates the mafia and lives off the income generated by the hard-working North. The Southern Italian views the Northerner as a semi-literate, half-Austrian or half-French peasant who, by accident of birth, dwells in the richest part of the country and lives off the income generated by the Southerners who work for him in his factories or on his land.

While both these pictures are exaggerated, enough Italians believe in them for the Northern League (a political party promoting a federalism that is not far from separatism) to be a serious force in Italian politics.

The difference in diet, habits and language between the two areas is sufficient to continually fuel these views. The Southern Italian diet was traditionally based on pasta and olive oil, whereas the Northern Italian one was based on maize, rice and butter. And the language variations can be so great that some of the southern dialects can hardly be penetrated by those from the North, and vice versa.

> **66 The Southern Italian diet was traditionally based on pasta and olive oil, whereas the Northern Italian one was based on maize, rice and butter. 99**

There is a real possibility of Northerners blaming everything they think is wrong in Italy, or that they don't like in the Italian character, on Southerners. So, for example, they see the corruption that riddles Italian politics and government as a 'southern disease', carefully ignoring the fact that the heart of Italy's greatest corruption and graft scandal, *tangentopoli*, was the great northern Italian city of Milan, and that the mafia has become increasingly powerful in the North.

The extremists of the Northern League and the Southerners who hark back to the golden years of the

South under the Kingdom of the Two Sicilies only exacerbate the problem: both conveniently forget that if all the Southerners went home, South Italy would be without the economic support of the Northerners, and North Italy would be without hairdressers.

A contradiction in terms

Italy is a country of contradictions. It is the country of the Catholic Church, but also of the mafia. It is the most pro-European country in Europe, but one of the worst at implementing EU directives. It has some of the world's most advanced engineering, but some of its most antiquated plumbing. It is a country of enormous wealth and of extreme poverty.

> **Italy is a country of contradictions. It has some of the world's most advanced engineering, but some of its most antiquated plumbing.**

As an American ambassador put it when he was returning home after completing his stint at Rome, 'Italy is a very poor country with a lot of very rich people living in it.' This opinion appears to be backed by statistics which state that Lombardy is among the richest regions in the European Union. But Italians like to think that they are poor and that the citizens of all northern European countries are much richer than they are, but just better at hiding their wealth.

Character

On stage

The Italians are great actors and their lives often appear to be one big act. Much of Italian life is spent in public, on show, and everyone knows the value of *bella figura* (cutting a fine figure). Whether they are shopping in the supermarket or modelling clothes, working in the office or directing the traffic, serving in a restaurant or going to see the doctor, Italians know how important it is to act the part, and look the part as well. They learn how to act when they are children and go on acting throughout their lives.

> **Italians know how important it is to act the part, and look the part as well.**

Because ordinary Italian life is lived on stage, Italian theatre often looks as if it is overacted – it has to be, to differentiate it from the high drama of real life.

You are what you wear

Great care is taken to wear the right clothes on the right occasion. This is never a casual choice – it is important to wear the proper clothes for the role you are playing. The station master must look like a station master. He must act the part too since he is on stage in the great film set of life. This is where style is so important. The taxi-driver, the teacher, the doctor, the lawyer and the engineer must all dress, act and behave like taxi-drivers, teachers, doctors, lawyers and engineers.

Taking life easy and being seen to take things easy, whether you are at the beach, in the disco or even at work, is part of *bella figura*, which explains why Italians are often happy to work in jobs that might seem very boring, such as lifeguards or security guards. There they can be on show all the time and be seen to be looking good and taking it easy – on the beach, or hanging around the bank looking important dressed up as a gunslinger. It doesn't matter that the job is not so pleasant in winter, nor whether the guard is actually able or even allowed to use the gun, as long as he looks the part.

> **66 Sports are often taken up just for the look. 99**

Nowhere can this be seen better than in the world of sport. It makes no difference if you can't swim very well, for that sub-aqua course you must have the right clothes and gear and style and you must look and act like a sub-aqua diver. This is why the latest fashion is important, for it makes your performance more convincing. Many Italian lofts are full of sportswear and gear, bought at great expense but abandoned because they are out of date or their owner has taken up another activity. In fact, sports are often taken up just for the look. Cross-country skiing enjoyed a boom when skin-tight Lycra ski-suits were invented. It was worth braving the freezing cold and the physical agony of this tiring sport for a couple of hours in order to be able to show off in the bar afterwards (and it might even have been good for your health, too).

Italians are very observant of how other people dress, particularly foreigners who are generally considered to dress badly. During the Second World War the Allied prisoners of war who managed to escape from prison camps had far more problems travelling in Italy than in any other country in Europe. The clothes they made from their uniforms, sheets and blankets often took in the Germans, but rarely fooled the Italians.

Status and success

Italian society is highly complex and, although at surface level the only real social divisions might seem to be based on wealth, in reality there are many others linked to a host of related factors, from family background to schooling to work, sport, religion and so on. Those who have money, even temporarily, may spend it and flaunt it where and how they like. They will be treated as potentates – as long as they have enough, of course.

The one thing that captures the imagination of Italian males far more than the dream of being a star footballer is owning a major football team. As a business, everyone knows it's unprofitable, but as an image-booster, it's the tops. It is not by chance that the Agnelli family (of Fiat fame) are at the helm of Turin's Juventus, and it was not sufficient for the highest flying *arrivista* (parvenu) of his generation and the wealthiest man in Italy, Silvio Berlusconi, to own major media networks; he had to buy A.C. Milan in order to be seen as a *real* success.

Allegria

Allegria is a general effervescence and delight in living that is not easy for the outsider to penetrate. It is linked to the joy of being and tends to involve sunshine, company and collective high spirits and it is why Italians so often seem to be laughing and smiling together. Even if things aren't going as well as they should be, people usually make

> **66** *Allegria* is linked to the joy of being and tends to involve sunshine, company and collective high spirits. **99**

an effort to put on a good show, especially in public. Being cheerful and looking happy can be an integral part of '*bella figura*'.

Allegria is infectious and not sharing in it is regarded as bad form. All those attending that big family picnic in the mountains will demonstrate *allegria* in a big way, roaring with laughter at Uncle Gianni's imitation of Aunt Rita sitting down on a cactus by mistake, even if they have heard the story countless times before.

The counterpart of *allegria* is a depressing form of melancholy and suffering that visitors are usually spared since it is often brought on by the damp, cold weather of late autumn, and coincides with the seasonal increase in prices and taxes. But generally speaking, the Italians try to look on the bright side of life – a positive outlook aptly illustrated by their touching salutation: 'May the saddest days of your future be the happiest days of your past.'

Behaviour

The art of getting by

Italians are past masters at *arrangiarsi* (getting by), and at home and in communities abroad have always been famous for their ability to make the best of their situation. This is due to the fact that, more often than not, they have to.

> 66 Italians are past masters at *arrangiarsi* (getting by). This is due to the fact that, more often than not, they have to. 99

For example, when the traffic is held up by two drivers having a long conversation because they haven't seen each other since the day before, those in the traffic queue will make the most of the moment by fiercely sounding their horns and hurling insults, or reading their newspapers, or making phone calls while using the rear-view mirror to preen.

When the new Euro currency was introduced in 2002, many shopkeepers ignored the official exchange rate and simply knocked off one zero (so that 1000 lire became 1.00 euro), thus doubling their profit at one stroke. More resourceful still was the action taken in the days of the lira when, through a mixture of governmental incompetence and bureaucratic venality, Italy suffered a shortage of small change. The Italians just shrugged their shoulders and used boiled sweets instead.

> **Italian life and power are based on a system of gifts and favours.**

Giving presents

The Italians are generous people, but their generosity should be accepted with caution since few presents in Italy come without strings attached. Italian life and power are based on a system of gifts and favours. The moment someone accepts a gift, he owes the giver a favour and has concluded an agreement that could last a lifetime. So when one Italian gives another a lift to the station or the phone number of a good eye specialist, sooner or later he might expect something back.

Driving

Driving is the area of his life where the Italian male feels he can properly express himself. Ask what he means by a good driver or a beautiful road and he will wax poetic. He will tell you that a good driver is one who drives at speed from A to B, ensuring the maximum pleasure and comfort of his passengers, not braking too often, not driving over bumps or holes but slaloming round them, driving, in short, like a Ferrari Formula One team member. A beautiful road is a wide, well-cambered road, which can be driven at high speed without any unsettling bumps for his passengers, in short, a race track; the narrow, scenic road winding through the mountains will not be considered a beautiful road.

> ❝ In Naples there are two kinds of traffic lights: those that are there for decoration and those that are merely a suggestion. ❞

Owners of new Alfa Romeos are recommended by the company's manual to drive in a certain way to get the best performance and life expectancy from their vehicle: they should not drive too close to the car in front, they should not accelerate or brake suddenly between traffic lights; they should not corner at high speed, and so on... In other words they should not drive as Italians.

Country bumpkins who drive in Italian cities need to be aware of two basic rules: vehicles with out-of-town plates are regarded as fair game by both local drivers and traffic police; and traffic police enforce the traffic laws as and when they wish. And should you be driving in Naples, it is wise to remember that there are only two kinds of traffic lights: those that are there for decoration and those that are merely a suggestion.

Driving in the countryside can be entertaining, too, particularly when you don't know where you're going. Italian sign painters specialise in artistic road signs designed not to help motorists, but to be appreciated as masterpieces of art by those who live nearby. Fortunately it is not easy to get lost in Italy, as long as you already know the way and remember that, despite the efforts of the autostrada administration to convince drivers that they do, not all roads lead to Rome.

> **❝ Italians convey genuine warmth and pleasure at seeing people again even if they have seen them that morning. ❞**

Manners

Italians are courteous people, and well mannered. Greetings are important and, since they are very physical, hand-shaking and kissing are the norm. They convey genuine warmth and pleasure at seeing people again, even if they have seen them the day before or even that morning. Kissing is on both cheeks and there are no taboos about men greeting each other this way. Hand-shaking has the added advantage of revealing that neither party is holding a weapon.

In some circles Italians will call one another *cara* and *tesoro* (dear and darling) at the drop of a hat. Yet before crossing someone's threshold they will ask '*Permesso?*' (May I have permission?). *Ciao* is an informal greeting used both on meeting and on departure. *Buongiorno* (Good day) is used for most of the day until a certain point in the late afternoon, when

> 66 'What did you do last night?' will be regarded as a nosy or even impertinent question, but 'What did you do yesterday evening?' won't raise any eyebrows at all. 99

people will greet each other with *Buonasera* (Good evening), as if the afternoon did not exist. They are much more rigid about the difference between evening and night, so 'What did you do last night?' will be regarded as a nosy or even impertinent question, but 'What did you do yesterday evening?' won't raise any eyebrows at all.

In Italy there are three possible forms of addressing others: the *tu*, *voi* and *lei* forms. The *voi* form has mostly fallen into disuse, and the *tu* form is used in the family, by young people with one another, by adults who know each other well, and by colleagues. *Lei* is employed in formal conversation which traditionally requires the use of surnames, though it is now more natural to mix these with first names. Thus the travel agent or mechanic might refer to her or himself as Maria Cristina or Sergio, but still call their customers Dottore Rossi or Signora Ferrari.

Strangers are addressed as *signor* and *signora*, *signora* being favoured even if the woman is technically *signorina* (an unmarried one). Professional titles are much more widely used than in Britain and America. *Dottore* is not just for medical doctors, but for any form of graduate; *professore* is not just for those at university, but the term for all teachers. *Maestro* is not only used for composers, but craftsmen and even judo teachers; *ingegnere* is very highly prized, reflecting the high status that engineering graduates enjoy. Professional or honorary titles are also often used for famous people, so Giovanni Agnelli used to be referred to as *l'avvocato* (the Lawyer) and Silvio Berlusconi is *il cavaliere* (the Knight). Nobody minds if the professional titles are not used in exactly the right way, as long as they flatter the recipient.

> **❝ Italians are incapable of saying sorry in the usual sense; if they are not sorry, they feel they don't need to say anything, and if they are sorry, they can say it in the confessional. ❞**

Grazie and *prego* are the mainstay of Italian manners, but it is not considered rude to ask for a coffee in a bar by saying in a loud voice, 'A coffee'; after all one is buying a service. Apology, however, is rare. Italians are incapable of saying sorry in the usual sense; if they are not sorry, they feel they don't need to say anything, and if they are sorry, they can always say it in the confessional.

Etiquette

Punctuality is only relatively important in Italy and the time is often treated as approximate. Being late for appointments is tolerated rather than welcomed – a quarter of an hour is acceptable, but half an hour is not. So university professors can turn up for their lectures up to a quarter of an hour after the scheduled start, but if they pass that deadline they might find the lecture theatre empty.

Italians could never be considered good at queuing: in fact the idea of standing in line tends to make them laugh. The scrummage that occurs while waiting to go on the chairlift at ski resorts, or to buy tickets for a football match or a concert, occasionally creates real problems. The introduction of number dispensers in places where the worst fights used to break out, such as a public office or a fish counter, helps. People enjoy collecting the tickets and like the implied 'fair play'. What could be fairer than arriving early at the office, getting a ticket, going out to do some shopping or to have a cappuccino and then returning to the office just in time for your number to be called.

> **66 Punctuality is only relatively important in Italy and the time is often treated as approximate. 99**

Gestures and topics of conversation

Italians are among the world's great communicators although their language is by no means widely spoken. This deficiency is more than compensated for by the famous use of their hands to communicate.

Italian gesticulation is so expressive and so extensively used that an online dictionary of Italian gestures has been developed by Italian Americans. The mere fact that the dictionary exists gives an idea of the vast complexity and range of expression of the Italians' use of gestures, from hand signals that are clearly rude, to others which aid and reinforce their conversation.

Topics for discussion can range widely but the main staple of dialogue with strangers (where sensitive issues like politics and religion are to be avoided at all cost) is sport and health, and above all food and its preparation. Every Italian will light up and be interested in new ways of cooking old dishes and discuss, at length, the quantity and quality of the ingredients, their availability and their price.

> **❝ Italian gesticulation is so expressive and so extensively used that an online dictionary of Italian gestures has been developed by Italian Americans. ❞**

Talking about the weather is considered trite and only deserving of conversations like those held in the condominium elevator – thus, thankfully, of limited duration.

Family Matters

The family is far and away the most important social, economic, organisational and political unit in Italy.

The nuclear family is divided into: the father, the head of the family, who thinks he does all the work and decision-making; the mother, who in actual fact does most of the hard work and takes all the important decisions; the sons, who are generally spoilt and never really learn how to compete efficiently; and the daughters, who are rarely spoilt and as a result are often far more capable than their brothers with whom they have to compete at a disadvantage from a very early age.

> **Family functions are occasions where the pecking order of power and wealth in the family is carefully evaluated.**

The extended family is a very large-scale social unit, including all possible relatives. It is seen at christenings, weddings, and funerals, and generally involves large numbers of people.

Family functions are occasions of enormous ostentation and generosity, where the pecking order of power and wealth in the family is carefully evaluated. An Italian will even go as far as to pretend to be seriously ill in order not to go to a second cousin's wedding where he fears he might cut a *brutta figura* if he hasn't enough money for an expensive present and a new suit.

The Italian family is a highly sophisticated network of patronage and power held together by a complex system of exchanging presents and performing favours. Going against the wishes of the family is hard and in reality so difficult for most Italians that few are inclined to try.

Women

Italian women are brilliant actresses. Although they are completely emancipated and behave exactly as they want, when and where they want, they go through life pretending that they are quiet and subservient and that Italian men rule the roost.

It is really only an act, for Italian women rule the family. Italian wives and girlfriends know that image is important to their men, so they let them

> **❝ Italian women are brilliant actresses. They go through life pretending that they are quiet and subservient and that Italian men rule the roost. ❞**

think they are big, macho, decision-makers. However, they also know that their menfolk have been so molly-coddled as children that they are able to do very little for themselves apart from looking good, drinking coffee, chasing women, and playing with the children's toys. Italian women know all this because they have always taken great care to pamper their male children, thereby rendering them almost completely dependent. The secret of power is handed on by one generation of Italian women to the next: faking subservience is a small price to pay for power in the family.

Mummy's boys

Italian males rarely leave the nest and, even when they do, these *mammoni* (mummy's boys) usually only move into the house across the road, or the flat next door. Statistics show that nearly 40% of Italians in their early thirties still live at home with their parents.

> 66 The Italian male grows up thinking his mother is the Virgin Mary, and so naturally he thinks he is Jesus, or God's gift to the world anyway. 99

Behind every great Italian man there is a great Italian woman, sometimes his wife or his mistress, but usually his mother. The Italian male grows up thinking his mother is the Virgin Mary, and so naturally he thinks he is Jesus, or God's gift to the world anyway, or to its womenfolk at least.

It is not surprising that Italian males find it very difficult to leave home. Their mothers make it hard for them to do so by making sure that their sons are so cosseted that they have no real wish to leave. Even when they are married, they continue to behave as if they aren't, taking their clothes home at least once a week for their mother to wash and iron. Why give up a life of luxury and financial security with a woman who treats you as the Son of God for an uncertain future with a woman who might ask you do things around the house that you have never learnt to do, like making your bed or drying the dishes?

An Italian minister of the economy coined a new term for young Italian adults who continue to live in their parents' homes: '*bamboccioni*'. In fact young Italians, both male and female, have hardly any choice. Not only is there little tradition of living away from home during their student years, but it is unusual to find decent jobs until they are well into their thirties.

> **Italian children must be both seen and heard. They must also be on show all the time.**

Furthermore, the absence of suitably priced accommodation makes it practically impossible for them to afford to move out. They find themselves caught in a trap; wanting to live on their own, but unable to leave the nest and under fire for not doing so. And the catch might not end there: these days a third of all Italian marriages end in divorce, in many cases because the wives feel unable to compete with the mothers of their *bamboccioni*.

Children

Italian children are allowed to be both seen and heard; in fact, they must be both seen and heard. They must also be on show all the time, except, of course,

66 At an early age Italian children develop the key skills necessary for 'getting by' and for performing on the great stage of life. 99

between 2 and 5 p.m., when they should be having their afternoon nap. All Italian children take a siesta, which means they are not too tired to take part in the *passeggiata*, the time when all over Italy people take to the streets, to see and be seen, after the sun has begun to lose its heat. Many Italians never lose the habit of taking an afternoon nap, which might explain why they and their children still seem to have boundless energy at midnight.

There is just one problem though: the number of *bambini* is on the decline. One explanation is the cost: designer baby clothes and foods can be a heavy burden on the family budget; another is that spending time with their children might cramp their parents' social style. So children are dressed as miniature adults and exposed to most aspects of adult life. They are welcomed at restaurants and expected to be present at all family activities and functions. They grow up much faster than their northern European peers and at an early age develop the key skills necessary for 'getting by' and for performing on the great stage of life.

Italians are on the whole wonderful with children, even with obstreperous and bug-ugly ones. As the old Neapolitan saying runs, '*Ogni scarrafone è bello a mamma soja*' – 'Every beetle is beautiful to its mother'.

Grandparents

Generally wielding the financial power and patronage within the family, *i nonni* (the grandparents) are careful to indulge their grandchildren and inculcate in them the importance of returning favours for presents, thereby ensuring that when they, in turn, become *nonni,* their families will look after them well.

Belonging to an Italian family is a cradle to grave contractual agreement.

Friends

The importance of friendship may be over-shadowed by the role of the family, but it plays a key role in Italian society. Italians are highly gregarious people and love belonging to groups or cliques. The idea of belonging to a group is seen as natural and essential.

'Real' friendships are usually formed early on in life, at school or with neighbours, and tend to be life-long and important. Groups of old friends are tight-knit and admit few new members. Other 'real' friends can be made at university, at work, playing sport, and so on, though these friendships should perhaps be considered 'useful' rather than 'real'. Adult Italians belong to a whole network of 'useful' friendships: the good dentist who will extract your teeth 'at half-price', the smart lawyer who will present your case 'free of charge', the lady in the bread shop who will always keep a loaf of your favourite bread. Then there are friendships you would be better off without, often linked to 'offers you can't refuse'.

> 66 Most adult Italians belong to a whole network of 'useful' friendships. 99

Visitors sometimes accuse the Italians of wearing their hearts on their sleeves, but this 'superficial' friendliness is often misunderstood. They are being treated as friends without anything but friendship being expected in return, something that Italians rarely grant each other. There are no strings attached: they will not be asked to help Salvatore's second cousin Concetta find a job when she comes to their country in the spring.

Home

The Italians are eminently practical, and everything must have its use. Italian homes tend to be small and beautifully looked after, with the number of rooms kept to a minimum. Guest bedrooms are rare – 'They can stay in a hotel, can't they?' Much of Italian life is lived in public, and so the home tends to be treated like a star's dressing room where Italians go to change and relax between acts. Most homes have one room where visitors can be welcomed which contains the best furniture and pictures. However, this is usually off-limits to the family and so infrequently used that in winter it is freezing cold – there seems no sense in heating it.

Many Italian families have a second or even third home, at the seaside or in the mountains. These are generally small, one- or two-room apartments with bunk beds where the whole family can sleep on holiday.

Land tends to be considered much too valuable for growing flowers (unless, of course, they can be sold), so Italian gardens

> **66 Outsmarting other Italians who can then be mocked as slow and gullible, is central to the Italian psyche. 99**

are often kitchen gardens. The Italians are brilliant at growing quantities of wonderful fruit and vegetables on tiny plots of land, or even on their balconies.

Obsessions

Outsmarting other Italians

Outsmarting other Italians, who can then be mocked as slow and gullible (or *fesso*), is central to the Italian psyche, and is generally regarded as a positive virtue, as long as it is successful. Thus Italians rather admire and even envy the clever dick (*il furbo*) who connives to get to the front of the traffic jam and then jumps the red light and goes roaring off ahead of everyone else.

If he is seen by the traffic police, chased and stopped, the *furbo* will then swear blind that his wife is about to give birth, and that he has to get home as fast as possible to get her to the maternity hospital, and go roaring off again, with a police escort. Anything goes in the pursuit of outsmarting others, from the bending of rules whenever possible, to telling fibs. Italians grow up knowing that they have to be economical with the truth. All other Italians are, so if they didn't play the game they would be at a serious disadvantage. They have to fabricate to keep one step ahead.

Not getting away with something is the main risk involved, but it is generally regarded as an acceptable one. After all, that ticket for shooting the lights might never need to be paid, especially if the driver's cousin who works in the police department reminds the traffic policeman that they both support the same football team and lets him know that the driver just happens to have a spare ticket for the big match on Sunday afternoon.

> **Italians grow up knowing that they have to be economical with the truth. All other Italians are, so if they didn't play the game they would be at a serious disadvantage.**

Losing face is considered far worse than being found out, and Italians will often make and accept a whole series of what seem to be completely unnecessary or highly improbable excuses in order not to be seen to be at fault. Convenient euphemisms like, 'I mislaid your phone number' or 'Your letter never arrived', are so much easier to say than admitting that you underestimated the importance of a swift reply, and thus appearing a complete *fesso*.

Avoiding tax

Italy has the greatest number of taxes and some of the highest rates of taxation in Europe, but this is not a problem because Italians are famous for not paying them. The government takes this into consideration when calculating their demands. This has led to some misunderstandings. When Trieste passed from the Austro-Hungarian Empire to Italy in 1918, the people paid the taxes they were asked to pay. The tax inspectors immediately asked them to pay double the next year, working on the principle that people never paid more than 50% of what they could pay.

> **❝ Italy has some of the highest rates of taxation in Europe, but this is not a problem because Italians are famous for not paying them. ❞**

By and large salaried workers are unable to avoid paying taxes as these are deducted at source. Freelancers and the self-employed, however, do their best to avoid declaring anything more than minimal earnings. This enables them to benefit from Italy's welfare system which is weighted in favour of those with lower incomes.

Servicing the Italian national debt is no easy job, and the government often has recourse to financial amnesties to bring in revenue; for example, a building amnesty permitted all those who had broken the laws relating to construction to regularise their position by paying a fine. These amnesties are quite successful in raising money, but the reverse side is that they tend to encourage others to risk breaking the law, so the cycle continues. They also help to explain speculative building, often executed with an almost total absence of planning permission, which has ruined some of Italy's most beautiful beaches.

> **It is estimated that up to a third of Italy's economic activity is carried out unofficially.**

It is estimated that up to a third of Italy's economic activity is carried out unofficially and so is outside the reach of the official statistics and thus, by implication, of the tax office. This *economia sommersa* (hidden economy) is made up of *lavoro nero* (black-work, i.e., moonlighting) at all levels (not only the plumber, but the surgeon and the accountant, too, will work *in nero* whenever possible) and of income from criminal activities (drug smuggling, cigarette smuggling, prostitution, bribes). It goes some way to explain why, though their country is always on the verge of bankruptcy, Italians manage to look so affluent.

Security – the key factor

Italians are obsessed with security. They have to be, for theft and burglary are rampant, especially in the big cities where pickpocketing, bag snatching and break-ins are too commonplace for comment. This is why Italians invest in wonderful alarm systems and padlocks, turning their houses and shops into miniature fortresses.

> 66 Love is taken very seriously by Italians and it is endlessly thought about and debated. 99

Yet there are often weak points. Incredibly well-secured doors will only be held in place by the flimsiest of hinges, and that car alarm, which is so sensitive even a light shower of rain will set it off, may never be switched on.

Love

Love is taken very seriously by Italians – 99% of all their songs are about love – and it is endlessly thought about and debated, for what is life without *amore*?

The debate covers a large number of key issues: What effect does falling in love have on your diet? Is love good for your health? Is love possible without sex? Is sex possible without love? Is universal love possible? And what about free love? Whole television series are devoted to couples in love, couples out of love, couples looking for love, children and love, elderly people and love, and so on. The subject has endless scope and involves the entire nation.

Whether or not Latins really are dynamic lovers, Italians bask in the glory achieved by their forebears and millions of people continue to think that they are. However, it seems that trying to live up to their reputation causes widespread problems. Long articles appear in the press quoting statistics on the high numbers of male Italians who suffer from impotence. Fortunately help is at hand with high performance wonder drugs like Viagra whose Italian sales are breaking all records. A restaurant in Naples even offers '*pizza di amore*', a pizza with Viagra sprinkled on top along with the cheese and olives.

> **❝ Whether or not Latins really are dynamic lovers, Italians bask in the glory achieved by their forebears and millions of people continue to think that they are. ❞**

Most verbal insults are related to sexual behaviour. Men will accuse women of free and easy sexual morals, calling them *puttana* (whore) and so on. Between men, it is a sister's or a mother's honour that is called into question. When and if women swear, they tend to attack the virility of men by calling them gay, old, or impotent.

Nevertheless, the legend of the Latin Lover lives on, bolstered by articles like the one reporting the comforting fact that Italian condoms are half a centimetre longer than those used in other countries.

Betrayal

Love is linked to another national obsession, betrayal. Betrayal, or rather fear of betrayal, is what keeps relationships passionate in Italy, and what is love without passion?

Magazines such as Italian *Cosmopolitan* regularly reveal that large numbers of Italian husbands betray their wives, and vice versa. Despite this, betrayal is still a dangerous game in Italy: enraged fathers, brothers, uncles and cousins will not think twice before resorting to violence to defend the honour of the family. Italians are famous for *la vendetta*, and many a blood feud is begun which will continue for generations, or at least until the original cause has long since been forgotten.

Privilege

Many Italians have special *privilegi* or belong to privileged groups or areas where they pay few taxes, or don't have to pay taxes at all. Semi-autonomous regions like the Aosta Valley are comparatively happy to remain Italian as long as they continue to receive vast subsidies from central government, only paying, for example, a quarter of the price the rest of Italy pays for petrol.

Members of Parliament in Italy and Italian Members of the European Parliament receive preferential treatment wherever they go. The same privilege is given to all those in positions of power and authority, from the members of the local council to the local chief of police. *Le autorità* (local dignitaries) can count on the fact that for anything that really matters – important football matches or concerts – they have a permanent reservation for the best seats.

Politics

Government

Italians have no real link or sense of connection to their government which is viewed as an alien, hostile organisation, hungry for the taxes that will go into the pockets of the current group of fat cats who are running it. It is also a convenient scapegoat for the nation's problems. An old political cartoon sums up the Italians' attitude. A man is standing on his doorstep looking out at the pouring rain. The caption reads: 'It's raining. The Government's a bunch of crooks.'

Italy has had 66 governments since the start of its First Republic in 1946, but until 1994 its politics were basically dominated by one political party, the Christian Democrats, kept in power by a coalition of allies. Cambio di governo was not so much a 'change of government' as a cabinet reshuffle. So, as it was always obvious who would win any election, the majority of Italians became used to being on the winning side. Much of the present uncertainty in Italian politics is that people are no longer sure which is the winning side.

Politicians

Italy is a country that seems to survive despite the efforts of its politicians to ruin it. The Italians love playing politics and the aim of the game is often difficult for foreigners to understand. One of the rules of Italian politics is that nothing that is said means exactly what it appears to, and de-codifying the speeches of the nation's leading politicians is an art form in itself.

> **66 Italy is a country which seems to survive despite the efforts of its politicians to ruin it. 99**

Politics permeates Italian life, and office or boardroom meetings can be fraught with tension. The most highly charged meeting of all is that held annually in every apartment building, the *riunione di condominio*. No holds are barred as administrators and homeowners spend hours heatedly debating whether the front façade should be redecorated. If you can survive one of these meetings success-fully and have actually enjoyed it, then you are proba-bly ready to become a rising star on the Italian politi-cal circuit.

Italian politicians are among the most highly paid in the world and, despite their heated public quarrelling, will often join together to protect the interests of their profession. So much so that they usually manage to survive any attempt at reform, not just with all their privileges intact, but with an increase in salary

> **66 Achieving power and patronage are regarded as all-important goals; a Sicilian saying runs 'Ruling is better than screwing'. 99**

to boot. It's a capacity for survival that has led them to become known as '*la casta*' (the caste).

Present-day politicians behave in much the same way as their ancestors. The power struggles, political corruption and clientalism that plagued the Late Roman Empire are alive and well in Italy today.

Achieving power and patronage are regarded as all-important goals; a Sicilian saying runs '*Comandare è meglio di fottere*' ('Ruling is better than screwing'). And yet, perversely, in Italian politics it is often con-sidered more important to destroy what your rivals are trying to build than to try and build something yourself.

Unfortunately (or perhaps fortunately), the Italian people, like the Roman mob of old, can still be kept happy and quiet with 'bread and circuses' and Italian politicians and leaders know this. It is no accident that Italy has one of the best football league championships in the world. Matches starring the world's most expensive football players have replaced the gladiatorial combats and displays in the Colosseum.

Left or right

The labels of Italy's political parties have often been very confusing. The Liberals were never particularly liberal, the Socialists not notably socialist, the Communists definitely not communist, and the Christian Democrats neither very Christian nor very democratic.

Italians, particularly those on the left, worry enormously about what should be labelled right- and left-wing. Debates take place over whether bodybuilding is right-wing, or whether employing a home help is left-wing, anxieties not lessened by the increasing

> **66 Italians worry enormously about what should be labelled right- and left-wing. 99**

awareness that it really makes little difference either way. And in the end, despite their great individuality, the Italians tend to follow the herd instinct. It was one of their own, Italian journalist Indro Montanelli, who said that they are *'pecore indisciplinate'* (undisciplined sheep).

Bureaucracy

All Italians believe that long bureaucratic procedures are of the utmost importance, but for *gli altri*, of course, not for themselves. Without these procedures other Italians would most certainly get up to every kind of mischief. Moreover, there are so many powerful interests involved in the Italian bureaucratic system it is unlikely that anything will change. The Italian state earns vast revenues from the fact that many bureaucratic or legal procedures involve *carta bollata* (taxable, officially stamped paper), and the same procedures also keep hundreds of thousands of civil

> 66 There are so many laws and ministerial directives in the Italian system that their strict application can more or less paralyse any bureaucratic procedure. 99

servants in gainful employment. The longer the bureaucratic process, the greater the number of people involved. Furthermore, without the long bureaucratic process, there would be no point in circumventing it, and the thousands of *galoppini* (unofficial specialists in accelerating bureaucratic procedures) would also be without employment.

There are so many laws and ministerial directives in the Italian system (it has been calculated that to be entirely in line with the law an Italian citizen should know some 800,000 rules), and they are so diverse, complicated and often contradictory, that their strict application can more or less paralyse any bureaucratic process. And because even minor civil servants wield considerable power in Italy to accept, refuse or delay requests or procedures, they are treated with enormous respect and courtesy, especially when they are wearing a uniform. Conversely, the officials 'become' their jobs when they are in uniform and expect to be treated with the kind of deference northern Europeans reserve for crowned Heads of State.

Italian bureaucracy needs to be approached tactically. If approached the wrong way, officials become intransigent and will make little or no effort to help you solve your problem. If approached the Italian way, they can be flexible enough to permit a solution to be found.

Every citizen knows that falling foul of the system by upsetting the wrong official, or not contacting the right middle man, could mean years of waiting. Officials can make your life easy or difficult, depending upon their whims. A Californian who was teaching at an Italian university wanted to enrol in some courses. To do so he went to

> **66** Every citizen knows that falling foul of the system by upsetting the wrong official or not contacting the right middle man, could mean years of waiting. **99**

the university admissions office and was told that he would need a copy of his university degree certificate, with a translation certified by the Italian consulate in Los Angeles. Having gone to California during the summer vacation and obtained the necessary certificate and translation, he returned to the admissions office. 'Ah, very good, now all we need is a copy of your high school diploma.' The Californian's protestations that obviously he couldn't have entered university without a high school diploma were of no avail.

> **66 While officials are treated with respect by Italians, this is not the case for places or objects that are public. 99**

According to the admissions office he had to return to Los Angeles, get it and have its translation certified by the Italian consulate there. In the end he was forced to do what he had wanted to avoid doing at the beginning, which was to ask one of his senior colleagues to do him a favour and intervene so that he could by-pass the official.

While officials are treated with respect by Italians, this is not the case for places or objects that are public. The Italian has no feeling that these things are his, and he should therefore treat them well. His house or flat will be spotlessly tidy and clean, but he will think nothing of leaving litter and rubbish on the pavement and street outside it; there they become the city council's responsibility, not his.

Referenda

From time to time the Italians are called upon to vote in referenda on important issues, such as divorce, abortion, nuclear power, the use of pesticides in farming and the number of television channels any one Italian citizen can own. This gives them a sense of being involved in political decision-making.

A referendum requires a 50% turn-out to be a valid quorum. Thus, despite an increasing number of Italians wishing to protect the country's ever-diminishing number of birds and beasts, a referendum on the issue only resulted in a 45% turn-out and new

66 Referenda give Italians a sense of being involved in political decision-making. 99

legislation was blocked. On the other hand, the population turned out in force to vote in favour of having television films and documentaries interrupted by commercials.

The mafia

Mafia is a word used all over the world both for criminal organisations and for coteries of power, so that people talk about a sports mafia, an arts mafia or a business mafia, yet the model is always the Italian mafia.

In Italy 'mafia' covers several different bodies each ruling over a well-defined territory, the main ones being the *Camorra* in the region around Naples, the *'Ndrangheta* in Calabria (the tip of the boot), the *Sacra Corona Unita* in Puglia (the heel), and the *Cosa*

Nostra in Sicily; but whatever the name, they mean the criminal organisation.

Mafia in all its local forms has for centuries been a way of life in the South of Italy – except for some for whom it has been a way of death. The reason for its success is simple enough: in the absence of a recognisable or effective government, it was the only organised system ordinary people could refer to when they needed, say, a permit to work or to get married.

Most Italians are terrified and fascinated by the mafia at one and the same time. They know its tentacles of power reach to the highest levels in politics and business since the mafia have always specialised in making offers that cannot be refused, knowing that everything and everyone has their price. They also know that the code of *omertà* (silence) is so strong that the odds are that the mafia will never be defeated, and every time one of its tentacles is lopped off, hydra-like others will grow again, stronger than before.

66 Italians know that the code of *omertà* (silence) is so strong that the odds are that the mafia will never be defeated. 99

The mafia is seen as a cancer that is slowly destroying the Italian state. The Italians have to live with it and alongside it, a state within a state, sharing their country with it as they always have done. And yet they secretly believe that, just as the right treatment in time might be able to cure a tumour, sooner or later a remedy will be found and administered in time to defeat the mafia.

Much of the time the mafia is divided, as its various families fight out their latest power struggle in time-honoured ways. Dark-suited men carrying violin cases still burst into barbers' shops in the back streets of Palermo and gun down the bosses of rival clans. Luckily, the closest most Italians will ever get to the real thing is the latest gripping episode of one of the many highly popular television series on Italy's organised crime, such as *Distretto di Polizia* (Police Precinct).

Leisure & Pleasure

The Italians live life to the full, and do not feel in the least bit guilty about leading a life of leisure and pleasure 24 hours a day, seven days a week, 52 weeks a year. This is what life is all about: Italians do not live to work, they work to live.

Shopping

One of their main leisure activities is shopping. Italians just love shopping. Their cities are full of wonderful craftsmen and skilled tailors, as well as shops catering for every taste and whim. The quality and luxury of the goods on display in the main streets is stunning. As

49

are the price tags. But although only the rich and famous will actually enter Prada, Gucci, Armani, Versace, Dolce & Gabbana and Valentino to buy, Italians are not put off for they know that the final price of the goods on display could turn out to be very different, especially when sooner or later they may turn up in the sales or in a street market.

Shopping is considered fun, especially at the markets where there are real bargains to be found, but one should never enquire too deeply into the provenance of the goods. As long as it fits, does it really matter that the beautiful little black Moschino cocktail dress being offered to you at 50 euros is the same as the one you saw for sale in the Via Veneto last night at 900 euros? Of course, the risk is yours, and that real bargain could just as easily be a real fake.

> **66 Italians will sell anything and everything, from their grandmother to their next-door neighbour – at the right price, of course. 99**

Haggling is acceptable in the markets, and customers are expected to ask for a discount in shops. Italians will sell anything and everything, from their grandmother to the Leaning Tower of Pisa – at the right price, of course. In Naples, for example, the street kids will unscrew your car number plate at one set of traffic lights and sell it back to you at the next with a smile and, naturally, at a bargain price.

Sport

In recent years rugby has begun to enjoy enormous popularity in Italy, but football is far and away the most important sport. Matches are played on Sunday afternoons and Italian men can often be seen plugged into the game as they take their family out for a Sunday afternoon stroll. When the national team is playing in the World Cup, the whole country comes to a halt and everybody forgets their regional differences – in front of the television. The only other sport taken seriously at a national level is cycling, and the progress of the Italian competitors in the *Giro d'Italia* and the *Tour de France* is followed with rapt attention – doping scandals notwithstanding.

> **66 Beautifully dressed Italian joggers are easily overtaken by the average walker. 99**

Because few Italian schools have good sports facilities the Italians do not grow up with much active sport apart from physical education classes and it is hard to find anyone participating seriously in sport. Beautifully dressed Italian joggers are easily overtaken by the average walker as they flaunt their way around the park on a Sunday morning.

Nevertheless, Italy regularly manages to produce world and Olympic champions in a whole variety of sports, from skiing and fencing to rowing and shooting, with both the competitors and their country relishing and making the most of every opportunity for occupying the centre stage.

Sense of Humour

Italians have a good sense of humour and are able to laugh at themselves as well as at others. But as they also have great respect for the role they are playing, they prefer not to ruin the effect with levity. They are very conscious of public dignity and, when playing an institutional part, will act it with great formality and aplomb. It's an attitude that explains why the law professor will not lard his lectures with wisecracks. This often means that Italian academic papers and conferences can be among the most serious and thus most tedious in the world. You might hear an occasional vein of discreetly veiled irony in the comments and presentation, but you have to listen hard for it.

> 66 As they also have great respect for the role they are playing, they prefer not to ruin the effect with levity. 99

Cartoonists satirise political figures and situations with devastating irony. Political cartoons in Italian newspapers have been honed to a keen edge because the crime of *vilipendio* – which makes those who insult politicians or public officials in writing liable to prosecution on criminal charges – does not include drawn illustrations. Italians enjoy seeing themselves through another's eyes, and they get a further running commentary in the press from Italian cartoonist, Altan, whose pithy observations on their character are sent from his comfortable perch in Brazil. Here are two examples:

Two builders wearing their origami hats (builders in Italy will fold a newspaper page into the shape of a boat, and wear it as a sunhat) are sitting on a pile of bricks having their lunch. One is reading an old newspaper: 'It says here that the Italians are a bunch of individualists.' 'Who cares?' says the other. 'That's up to them.'

A conversation between two young women, reflecting on the antics of their lovers: 'One has to admit that Italian men are extraordinary,' says one. 'Definitely,' says the other, 'I only wish they were ordinary.'

The Italians' avid interest in keeping an eye on their neighbours is reflected by their humour, which has few jokes about other nationalities, but lots about other Italians. For example, one that reflects their belief that the people from Genoa are generally regarded as being stingier than the Scots:

Having decided to hang a picture in the living room, a Genoese father says to his son, 'Go and ask the neighbours if we can borrow their hammer.' The boy returns empty-handed: 'They say they're sorry but they can't find it.' 'That's bloody mean of them,' says the father. 'OK, go and get ours, then.'

Culture

The Italians have enormous respect for culture. They know the value of their national heritage and appreciate that it is one of the main sources of their country's wealth.

Money is, and always has been, a driving force behind Italian creative art, but it is not the only one. Religion, a sense of beauty, and a gift for understanding the spirit of place are also important. Perhaps the most important of all is the Italian's innate pride in making some-

66 Things don't necessarily have to work well, they don't necessarily have to last, but they do have to look good. 99

thing beautiful. In Italy, things don't necessarily have to work well, they don't necessarily have to last, but they do have to look good. And if they are beautiful, the Italians will make the effort to make them work well and to make them last. This is the link between a dress by Valentino, a car by Pininfarina, a glass gondola blown in a small workshop on one of the islands in the Venetian lagoon, a roadside Madonna and Child, and a plate of fresh pasta.

An example of this is even found beyond the confines of Italy. Italian prisoners of war on the Orkney Islands during World War II were given a Nissen hut to use as their chapel. They carefully decorated the inside, painting it with baroque trompe l'oeil and turning it into a work of art. Its fame and moving history draw tens of thousands of people each year.

Melodrama

Italian life is, and always has been, melodramatic, which helps explain the popularity of operas of the 19th century and soap operas of today. Plumbers can be heard singing well-known arias while they work, and cleaning ladies save their pennies for a ticket to dress up to the nines and attend La Scala. Karaoke enjoyed an incredible boom in Italy, giving ordinary Italians a wonderful opportunity to satisfy their narcissism by being 'on show'. What could be more fun than singing your heart out in front of your friends and family?

Television

If the Italians didn't actually invent trash television, they have certainly developed it to a fine art. Even on the three national channels there is a lack of finesse that would be considered really slapdash anywhere else. Viewers are often treated to completely blank screens, programmes regularly start later than scheduled and newscasters are frequently caught reading items that bear no relation to what is screened.

Italian viewing is mainly made up of films, cartoons and soap operas, which have been imported and dubbed. The dubbing is idiosyncratic: in the love scene from *A Fish called Wanda*, even John Cleese's utterances in Russian, which were supposed to excite Jamie Lee Curtis to a frenzy, were rendered into Italian.

On the other hand, the astonishing success of second-rate American soap operas in Italy is largely due to the real passion of the Italian versions, where the dubbing has served to cover up the poor quality of the original dialogue. The Italian version of *The Bold and the Beautiful* resulted in its little-known American stars achieving cult status in Italy and being better known than some of the members of the government.

> **66 The astonishing success of second-rate American soap operas in Italy is largely due to the real passion of the Italian versions. 99**

Most home-grown productions are variety shows which cater for so-called 'family viewing' and as Italian children are usually still up and about at 10.30 p.m., they tend to go on interminably all evening, offering the same basic ingredients of quizzes, games and competitions interspersed with song and dance routines and advertisements. The first Italian *Big Brother* (*Grande Fratello*) was enormously successful, the ninth and tenth far less so as the novelty wore off. Other highly successful programmes include the various talk shows in which ordinary people air their personal problems, which are then discussed at length. The problems focus on the national obsessions of love and betrayal, food and football, health and security; and the more heated the debate, the higher the audience ratings seem to rise.

The alternatives for family viewing are dubbed Walt Disney imports and wildlife documentaries. Despite being great Europeans, when it comes to light music the Italians prefer their own song contest to the Eurovision Song Contest. It is held in the city of San Remo on the Riviera every February, lasts most of the week and draws huge television audiences.

> **Talk show problems focus on the national obsessions of love and betrayal, food and football, health and security.**

Other programmes take their cue from *Candid Camera* and give viewers the chance to see unwitting participants reduced to tears and rage without knowing they are being watched by an audience of millions. In *Complotto di Famiglia* (Family Conspiracy) for instance, Maria accompanies her husband to an important business dinner for the first time. As the evening progresses, it becomes increasingly clear that the glamorous hostess in a tight pink suit is paying too much attention to Maria's husband. At a certain point she asks Maria to 'lend her husband to her for a bit'. The husband seems to acquiesce and the ensuing scene is fraught with anguish and emotion.

However, the programme ends before viewers can see whether or not Maria and her husband manage to save their marriage.

Late-night viewing is for adults only, and 'high quality' films compete with strip shows where 'housewives' take their clothes off to win prizes.

Among the most successful programmes are the gameshow, *Affari tuoi*, the Italian version of *Deal or No Deal,* and a programme called *Striscia la notizia*, which devotes half an hour each evening to investigating complaints made by callers, as well as showing and commenting on a cunningly edited collation of recently televised news and events adorned by two skimpily-clad showgirls whose outfits just manage to stay on during their dance routines. Presented in this way it combines titillation with a daily dose of two of the things Italians enjoy most in life – debunking their politicians and laughing at others' mistakes.

> 66 Late-night viewing is for adults only, and 'high quality' films compete with strip shows where 'housewives' take their clothes off to win prizes. 99

Literature

Italy has a fine literary heritage. Famous writers from the past include Dante Alighieri, Boccaccio and Ariosto, while amongst the recent and current are

Primo Levi, Italo Calvino, Alberto Moravia, Umberto Eco and Dario Fo. Their works tend to be looked on as 'great literature' and, as such, are usually reserved for studying at school, or appreciating on special occasions. For more general reading, on trains or in bed, the Italians enjoy racy, international, best-selling blockbusters such as Wilbur Smith, Danielle Steel and Dan Brown.

Some literary genres are colour-coded. Yellow is used for thrillers and detective stories, black for the *cronaca nera* or crime pages in newspapers and magazines, and pink for romantic novelettes.

> **Perhaps the most successful literary genre in the country which gave the world that much-loved children's character, *Pinocchio*, is the comic.**

Italians are not great readers. This seems to be partly due to the educational system, but mostly due to the ubiquitous television screen: it is hard to read a book and watch television at the same time, and in many houses the television set will be blaring all day and most of the night too.

Perhaps the most successful literary genre in the country which gave the world that much-loved children's character, *Pinocchio*, is the comic. Italians adore book-length comics. They are often happiest of all reading the soft porn adventures of their imaginary heroes, like cowboy *Tex Willer*, sexy fashion victim *Valentina,* and the off-beat investigator of nightmares and inveterate womaniser, *Dylan Dog.*

Customs & Tradition

Christmas is traditionally celebrated at home with the family, and Easter is spent with friends: '*Natale con i tuoi, Pasqua con chi vuoi*' (Christmas with your own, Easter with whomever you want). But Easter Monday (called *Pasquetta*, little Easter) always involves a big family picnic. Never mind that it often rains on Easter Monday (the weather having changed with the Easter moon), this picnic is rarely called off.

> **❝ People take time off to do what Italians enjoy most, eating good food and drinking good wine at a leisurely pace in good company. ❞**

Every Italian town and village celebrates its own saint's day. Milan takes the day off for St. Ambrose, Turin for St. John, Naples for St. Gennaro and Rome for St. Peter.

Most places also have a *sagra* or festival week devoted to a composer, or food, or a sports event, or an award named after some local poet or politician. These can be on the grand scale, like the great *palio* (horse race) at Siena, but often they are local affairs, where the people take time off to do what Italians enjoy most, eating good food and drinking good wine at a leisurely pace in good company.

Annual holidays in Italy are mostly taken in August, when the factories in the great northern cities close as the heat of the summer makes city life unbearable, and most families head for the mountains or the seaside to cool down. Life becomes difficult for those who stay behind, as the shops close too, and it isn't always easy to find the basic necessities of life, while those on holiday do their best to recreate the hustle and bustle of city life on the beach.

Other important holidays in Italy include 8th March, when women exchange yellow mimosa and celebrate International Women's Day, 1st May, when half the country is

> **66 Those on holiday do their best to recreate the hustle and bustle of city life on the beach. 99**

involved in Don Camillo-style first communions and the other half in Peppone-style workers' parades, and 1st November (All Saints Day), when most Italians take part in serious ancestor worship, visiting their dead in the cemeteries where they repose in multi-decker tombs, stacked one above the other, like so many filing cabinets.

The days before Ash Wednesday, when the abstinence of Lent begins, are dedicated to celebrating Carnival (from the Latin *carnem levare* – literally 'put away meat'), with fancy dress parades and parties climaxing in the Shrove Tuesday (*Martedì Grasso*) festivities, the biggest of which take place in Venice and Viareggio. The Italian Carnival dates back to the pagan Roman feasts of Saturnalia and Lupercalia. For some, Carnival is a time for dressing up as Harlequin or Pulcinella, or dressing up their children and taking them to the parade and the funfair; for others it is a wonderful excuse for behaving outrageously. But Italy's traditions are no closed shop: in recent years Halloween has enjoyed enormous popularity as shop windows have filled up with hollowed out pumpkins and whole neighbourhoods have been taken over by miniature witches and wizards.

The Catholic church

The Italians like to think that Italy is a Catholic country, even if they are highly irreverent towards their clergy and tend to ignore papal diktats, such as those concerning birth control (despite the Vatican's line, Italy has the lowest birth rate in Europe, with an average of 1.2 children per family). Italians can be very ambivalent about their religion.

The exact role of the Catholic Church in present-day Italy is hard to quantify. Superficially its power is on the wane, yet in terms of real power it might even be stronger than in the past. It is present in every parish and in every community.

66 Superficially the church's power is on the wane, yet in terms of real power it might even be stronger than in the past. 99

Pope John Paul II had an enormous personal following among the nation's young as was demonstrated by a celebration at the height of the holiday season in Millennium year when around a million young people gathered in a field to hear him say mass and to sing a few hymns together. Despite scorching heat and being kept waiting for hours, it was agreed by all to have been a truly memorable occasion, far more fun than most rock concerts. His German successor Joseph Ratzinger, despite his nationality, was treated with respect – after all, as one of Italy's journalists commented, all Italians are Christian at heart whether they go to church or not. Yet deference for his papal dignity did not prevent some of the biggest Italian fireworks on sale for New Year's Eve being nicknamed *ratzingers* (the Italian for missiles is *razzi*).

> **Religion is preferred to be visual and tangible, hence pictures of the Madonna, the Pope, local saints and football stars are pasted everywhere.**

Religion is preferred to be visual and tangible, hence pictures of the Madonna, the Pope, local saints and football stars are pasted everywhere – in public places, private homes, and even on personal computers.

The Pope (*il Papa*) is Italy's only crowned Head of State and because of his position his visits to Italian cities are treated with much greater interest and excitement than those of the President or the Prime Minister. He is the only leader in Italy who can fill a stadium with his fans, and the only visitor *le autorità* will make an effort to impress, painting the stadium walls white on the morning of his visit, so that no offensive graffiti will offend his holy eyes.

Superstition

The Italians worry about objects, events, behaviour and (especially) people who they think cause, or might cause, them misfortune. Many protect themselves, their cars and their houses with an array of prayers and amulets, and spend huge amounts of money visiting a whole series of astrologers, witches and charlatans, as a kind of insurance policy against 'the evil eye'.

They also make good practical use of their superstitions. An Italian had a dream that he was sitting with Pope John XXIII listening to an old 33 r.p.m. record. When he woke up he told the dream to his neighbour. Her first reaction was: '23 and 33. I'll play those numbers on the Lotto (national lottery) tomorrow.'

> **The Italians worry about objects, events, behaviour and (especially) people who they think might cause them misfortune.**

The number 13 is held to be lucky by some Italians, unlucky by others, and in Italy a cat only has seven lives, not nine. By contrast, the number 17 is considered very unlucky in Italy: the most plausible explanation is that when written as the Roman numeral XVII, it is an anagram of *vixi*, the Latin for 'I lived', with its implication that I no longer do.

Many people watch the cycle of the moon carefully, not just because of its effect on the human mind and body, but because of the effect it has on the sowing and harvesting of crops, and on the preservation of food and drink. Thus wine should always be bottled under the right moon; luckily it can be drunk under any moon.

Whether they are church-goers or not, Italians are fascinated by the unsolved mystery element of miracles. When an ordinary mass-produced statue of the Madonna started to cry tears of blood in a back-garden in Civitavecchia in spring 1995, the whole nation became involved in the debate ('Why

> **66 Church-goers or not, Italians are fascinated by the unsolved mystery element of miracles. 99**

did the bishop accept the miracle before the Vatican did?' 'Why was the blood male?' and so on), and *le autorità* and tradespeople got ready to handle the armies of pilgrims who were expected in the city. In the event, common sense prevailed and only a handful of locals actually showed up at the scene.

However, this is the country with the most impressive reliquaries in Christendom; the country of Padre Pio; the country where the blood of San Gennaro in Naples has liquefied three times a year since 1389. Never mind that there are enough pieces of the True Cross around to build a basilica, or that St. Eulalia (the foster mother of Christ) must have had 13 breasts, relics and miracles are good for keeping the faithful in the fold. Better still, they are good for business.

The Eat-alian Way

The Italians are foodcentric people. Much of Italian life revolves around the growing, buying, preparing and, above all, eating of food. Whenever possible, meals are shared and eaten in company. The very word 'company' comes from two Italian words, *con* (with) and *pane* (bread), implying breaking bread in friendship.

> **66 Italian enthusiasm knows no bounds when it comes to arranging a meal. 99**

But the Italian meal in company is much more than breaking bread, for Italian enthusiasm knows no bounds when it comes to arranging a meal. First there must be the *antipasti* (starters), usually a minimum of five, then the first course (the *primo*), with a choice of different pasta or rice dishes; next the main course (the *secondo*), which will be meat or fish with the accompanying vegetables (the *contorno*); then cheese, and finally the dessert (the *dolce*) followed by coffee (*espresso*). The meal can happily take from two to five hours to consume. If it is lunch, you have a couple of hours to recover before supper time.

Food

The Italians have always appreciated quality and keep the very best of foods for themselves. Italy is still an agricultural nation and its small farmers (*i contadini*), who wield enormous power in the community, are highly practical men. They pay little attention to EU directives and farm according to time-honoured ways, harvesting wonderful produce.

Many city-dwellers have relatives in the countryside who will keep them stocked up with home-grown and home-produced specialities. The salad and wine that are put on the table in honour of a guest will be very special, and every bite and drop will be truly memorable.

> **66 A look at Italian cook books shows that the writers start from the premise that their readers already know how. 99**

The Italians acknowledge the changing of the seasons and the different delicacies linked to each. The whole family will take part in preparing the *passata di pomodoro* (tomato purée) in the late summer, go mushrooming in September, grape-picking in October, and in March collect those exquisite young dandelion leaves that add a zest to salads.

The secret behind Italian cooking lies not only in the fact that the ingredients are fresh and of good quality, but also that most Italians, male and female, are excellent cooks. They learn how to cook when young, and a look at Italian cookbooks shows that the writers start from the premise that their readers already know how.

Italian recipes are much less precise than British or American ones and don't say, 'carefully add 150 grams of this' or 'slowly pour in 4 fluid ounces of that'; they simply say, 'take a pinch of this', or 'add a couple of drops of that'.

Despite their admiration for many things American, the Italians have been remarkably resistant to some American foodways. Coca-Cola and hamburgers have been accepted, but peanut butter and baked beans have not; breakfast cereals are advertised, but without much success. Italy is the only country in the world where the marketing strategies of McDonald's have been hampered by the highly successful Slow Food Movement.

> **What really runs in the nation's veins is wine. Country wines vary from the regal to the robust, each with its own distinct character.**

Grain, grape and *grappa*

Italians are the world's largest consumers of whisky, especially malt whisky – an average bar in Italy will stock a greater selection than most pubs in Scotland – and beer is becoming fashionable with the young, especially if it is strong and imported. But what really runs in the nation's veins is wine.

Italian wines range from purple-black table wines frothing in your glass to sparkling dry whites. They are generally drunk locally and young, and the fact that many of the best Italian wines are unknown outside Italy serves to keep their prices reasonable. Country wines vary from the regal to the robust, each with its own distinct character. As a village salami-maker remarked as he savoured a glass of his region's *vino nero*: 'A wine is like a man; it can have flaws and still be pleasing.'

66 On the whole, Italians drink only when they eat, but this does not mean that they stint themselves. 99

On the whole, Italians drink only when they eat, but this does not mean that they stint themselves. The meal will be preceded by an *aperitivo*, and each course will be accompanied by a different wine, with a sparkling wine reserved for the dessert.

Unfortunately, the human stomach was not designed for such conspicuous over-indulgence, so the Italians have thought up a variety of ingenious ways to help their digestive system cope. They drink mineral waters throughout the meal, and after it can choose from a host of evil-tasting medicinal preparations called *digestivi*, or perhaps a fiery *grappa*, in the hope that this will spur their jaded innards into action.

Despite these precautionary measures, the hard work that Italian digestive systems are asked to perform often leads to their going on strike, and constipation is a common complaint. Other nations' remedies are suspect, and Italians refuse to eat the German-style wholemeal breads and American-style high fibre cereals which might solve their problems, in much the same way as they refuse to change their eating habits, by eating, for example, a little less.

Health

The most common Italian illness is hypochondria. Italians are in general fairly healthy people who spend a great deal of their time thinking that they should feel healthier than they do. This is partly because they imagine that everyone else feels better than they do, and partly because they have absurd expectations about their own health. They worry constantly about it. Could that stomachache be the beginnings of a peptic ulcer? – forgetting that they ate too much the night before. Might that headache be the beginnings of a brain tumour? – forgetting that they drank too much the night before.

> 66 Italians are in general fairly healthy people who spend a great deal of their time thinking that they should feel healthier than they do. 99

Italians are always eager to tell friends and neighbours about their preoccupations at length, so that animated exchange you witness as you pass may as well be about piles as politics. The listener may not be quite so happy to be targeted, and when health bores have run out of friends and neighbours they may be obliged to button-hole any available stranger.

People are happy to spend vast sums of money servicing their hypochondria. If their doctor tells them they are in the pink of health, they will go to a private specialist. If this specialist finds nothing wrong, they will go to another one, and so on, until they find a doctor who is prepared to prescribe for them. The prescription will then be taken to the local chemist and discussed at length,

> **66** The typical Italian bathroom cupboard is crammed with as many medicines as most dispensaries. **99**

before the medicine is bought (and one or two others that the chemist has recommended as well; after all, you never know…). Consequently, the typical Italian bathroom cupboard is crammed with as many medicines as most dispensaries, most of them years beyond their expiry date.

Problems can occur when Italians are genuinely ill. They have already exhausted their doctor's patience and precious time, and they have already visited half the specialists in town. One possible solution is the hospital Casualty Department. But is that ingrowing toenail a serious enough ailment? Or might the hospital surgeon remove the wrong toenail in his zeal? Italian news reports are full of hospital horror stories, like the one about the Franciscan friar who went into hospital for a hernia operation and came out with only half his trachea. Or the footballer who had the wrong knee operated on. Despite the fact that there is little real evidence of Italian hospitals being any better or worse than those of other European countries, Italians will often travel to Switzerland or France for treatment, in the unshakeable belief that hospitals function better elsewhere.

Dental care

Most Italians look wonderfully fit and healthy, until they open their mouths. Dental treatment in Italy is very expensive and, unfortunately for them but fortunately for their dentists, Italians tend to wait until they have serious problems with their teeth before making an appointment. Rather than investing in continuous maintenance, they treat their teeth as they do their ancient monuments, waiting until they are almost beyond repair. Why bother to do a temporary fixing when you could wait until there is a really big job to be done?

Business

The Italian industrial and financial system seems to suffer constantly from the after-effects of some major scandal, such as those resulting in the collapse of food chain giants Cirio and Parmalat; and those involving a bungled attempt to prevent two of Italy's banks from being taken over by the Dutch and Spanish. Nevertheless, the same policy can be successful, especially if it is seen as being in the national interest and is backed by enough members of *la casta*.

Italy is full of interest groups, such as the cartels that run the world of finance and banking and the guild-like associations that dominate the professions and trades, from the lawyers to the accountants, from the engineers to the taxi drivers, guaranteeing their monopolies and privileges. The trade unions are similarly obsessed with the preservation of the interests of their increasingly elderly membership (over 50% of the paid up members of Italy's largest trade union, the CGIL, are pensioners). These powerful interest groups have their own lobbies and, as they often join together to defend their privileges, they make serious reforms practically impossible.

> **66 Powerful interest groups have their own lobbies and, as they often join together to defend their privileges, they make serious reforms practically impossible. 99**

Business in the private sector in Italy is dominated by a handful of leading families, such as Agnelli (cars), Pirelli (tyres), Del Vecchio (eyeware), Della Valle (shoes), Berlusconi (TV channels) and Benetton (clothes). Although their companies are, in fact, vast conglomerates with a wide diversity of interests, they are run as family businesses rather than multi-national corporations. Power tends to be kept within the family group by a series of cross-holdings. There is no similar concentration of power in any other western country.

The success of the Italian economy is based on the skills, hard work and dynamism of the small and medium-sized companies in the North that produce a large part of the country's GNP. They are mostly family-run businesses, organised in such a way as to minimise the payment of taxes and national insurance contributions. Italy is perhaps the only country in the world where employees appear to earn more than their employers, or so it would seem from their tax declarations. Similarly, professional people and craftsmen, like accountants, goldsmiths, dentists and lawyers, have few qualms about declaring subsistence level earnings while maintaining two or more houses, a racehorse and three yachts.

> **66** Italy is perhaps the only country in the world where employees appear to earn more than their employers, or so it would seem from their tax declarations. **99**

The Italian job

Every Italian mother dreams that her children, especially her male children, will achieve *lo starbene* – a state of physical and mental well-being in their work. What this generally entails is finding *lavoro fisso* (a steady job) in the air-conditioned office of a government department or government-owned bank or company, and looking good behind a big desk. Though not particularly well-paid, these jobs entitle their holders to 13 or even 14 months' salary a year and offer all sort of perks including almost total job security and the possibility of retiring early on a full pension. Best of all, they are usually so undemanding that their holders can concentrate most of their energies on the family business, or on whatever really interests them: watching football, collecting stamps or just sitting, sipping coffee, reading comics. Too bad

> **In the public sector some offices are only open to the public for two hours a week, and others are never open at all.**

that the *lavoro fisso* is becoming ever harder to find as the Italian system falls into step with work practices elsewhere in the European Union, but it still remains the objective of most young Italians and, of course, their mothers.

Life in the average Italian office is like Italian life in general. Style and behaviour are important, and managerial and office staff should, of course, look and act the part. Punctuality has been taken a little more seriously since the advent of clocking in and out of work. Office hours can be very long in the private sector (8.00 a.m. – 7.30 p.m. with only half an hour for lunch). However, things are very different in the public sector: some offices are only open Ito the public for two hours a week, and others are never open at all.

Many of the public holidays that Italians took in the past have been surrendered to EU rules, so the practice of *ponti* (building 'bridges' between the weekend and a national holiday) has assumed greater importance. Holidays are planned long in advance so as to be able to link them to public holidays. This is why Italian strikes usually take place on Mondays or Fridays.

> **66** Strikes in Italy reveal Italian passion, patience and resourcefulness at its collective best. **99**

Strikes in Italy reveal Italian passion, patience and resourcefulness at its collective best. The *autostrada* and railways will be occupied, rubbish not collected and hunger strikes started – to the point where the nation will seem to be on the verge of chaos – and then an unexpected compromise will be reached when none seemed possible. Everyone will claim victory, no-one will be seen to lose face, and the situation will return to normal. Everybody will have enjoyed the strike.

As always, their ability to 'get by' carries the day. When the La Scala orchestra went on strike on the opening night of the 1995 season, the conductor had a grand piano brought on stage and he and the soloists performed the whole concert without the orchestra, to rapturous applause.

Patronage

Patronage, or *raccomandazione*, along with its trading of favours, jobs and influence, is part and parcel of Italian business life. At its worst it prevents things from growing in a healthy way; at its best it is a kind of old boy network that is necessary in a country where little, in terms of real qualifications, is quite what it seems.

> **Patronage along with its trading of favours, jobs and influence, is part and parcel of Italian business life.**

In order to ensure fair play in the distribution of jobs in the public sector, and in an attempt to curb the problem of *raccomandazione*, the Italian authorities organise job competitions, when jobs are advertised and then candidates sit an exam to decide who are the most suitable for the position. When there are not too many candidates the system works reasonably well, but when 14,000 people applied to become refuse collectors in the region of Lombardy, the situation became more challenging. Undismayed, *le autorità* took over the local football stadium for the day and brought in desks and chairs from the schools.

Never mind the fact that the 'recommended' candidates will probably have been told the questions beforehand and that the great majority of candidates will be cheating as hard as they can, justice must not so much be done as be seen to be done.

Raccomandazione is closely linked to the political

'spoils' system of handing out jobs to supporters. The ministers in Silvio Berlusconi's 2008 cabinet included his tax lawyer (Giulio Tremonti – Economy), his children's ski instructor (Franco Frattini – Foreign Affairs) and a show girl from one of his TV channels (Mara Carfagna – Equal Opportunities).

Systems

Education

Compared with the educational systems of other countries, the Italians seem to have got theirs the wrong way round. In the country of Maria Montessori, Italy's best schools are probably its pre-schools, after which things seem to gradually regress through elementary, middle and high schools into a somewhat disorderly university system.

Small children spend most of their day at school, but as they get older schooling becomes limited to mornings only. High schools are specialised and students study a variety of classical, scientific and technical subjects, depending on the specialisation they have chosen.

Admission to Italian universities is comparatively easy and, since few faculties restrict the number of students enrolling on courses, vast numbers enrol. The University of Rome, for example, is the largest in the

European Union. As a result, courses are overcrowded and facilities inadequate. The fact that under a quarter of all those who matriculate in the universities actually graduate is perhaps a fair reflection of the inherent problems. In recent years large numbers of those who do graduate have found work abroad, often in research, to such an extent that the issue has been raised in Parliament, aiming to prevent this '*fuga dei talenti*' (brain drain) and to provide incentives for the researchers to return to Italy.

> **Few faculties restrict the number of students enrolling on courses, vast numbers enrol.**

Despite the idiosyncrasies of the system, or perhaps because of them, many Italians are very well-educated. They like the idea of studying and spend hours/weeks/months slaving over textbooks, highlighters in hand, learning the key sentences and concepts by heart. They are then tested in the oral exam, the *interrogazione,* parroting all they have learned. Critical comment by students is not welcomed. A repetition of the teacher's or professor's own views and pronouncements is regarded as the best approach – a hangover from the Counter-Reformation when the wrong answer might have led you to the stake.

There are no limits to the number of times students can take exams, and some will refuse to accept a mark they don't consider good enough. As the only limitation to staying at the university is the payment of annual fees, some students continue studying well into middle age. Life-long learning is no novelty in Italy.

Examinations are mostly oral (perhaps because cheating is so rife in written exams). This is because Italians fear that the other candidates in an exam will cheat, so they have to cheat too. Cheating is considered more or less acceptable, but being caught cheating is not.

Transport

In spite of the country's difficult terrain and crowded cities, Italy's public transport system is generally quick and efficient. The Italian autostradas and rail network are among the most impressive feats of engineering in Europe, passing under mountains and over river valleys to link the various parts of Italy.

Trains usually run to schedule, despite the absence of an authoritarian government. One of the dictator Mussolini's more successful moves, and perhaps the only one he is universally remembered for, was persuading people that his government improved the efficiency of public transport. However, to no-one's surprise, research has since proved that his government had little or no impact on this at all, with trains being just as punctual in the periods before and during his regime as after it.

Crime & Punishment

All Italians are individually perfect, but all Italians know that *gli altri* are imperfect. So Italian criminal law starts from the premise that you are guilty until you are proved innocent.

Italian criminals have few worries because the chances of being caught are very slim. The perpetrators of 83% of all

> **❝ Italian criminals have few worries because the chances of being caught are very slim. ❞**

crimes committed have yet to be brought to book, including 97% of theft, 64% of homicide, 86% of robbery and 72% of kidnapping. Punishment tends to involve either fines or imprisonment or both. Although Italian prisons are generally overcrowded and not particularly pleasant places to spend time, they are more comfortable than those in northern Europe and the United States. Indeed, conditions for imprisoned mafia bosses are said to be pretty cushy, and are regularly criticised in public for being so.

Italians are naturally gifted as con men. They are expert copiers and counterfeiters, and have long dominated the traffic in art works. The fact that there is no guarantee that the works are the real thing, and may well be stolen or faked by a craftsman, only adds to the spice of the trade. Whether the buyer is looking for a Roman vase or a Modigliani sculpture, the illegal Italian art world will find him what he wants.

Italian politicians have themselves set the example of corrupt behaviour by accepting vast bribes for fixing government contracts. The Italians chose to ignore this until the government of the day was caught in the act – thus changing status in a flash from *furbo* to *fesso*.

The police

There is a different police force for every occasion in Italy. There are national police, local police, traffic police, military police, financial police, railway police, secret police, private police, and so on.

The *carabinieri* are the most evident of Italy's police forces. Indeed, they are often involved in military as well as police activities. Despite the fact that it is extremely difficult to join their ranks, and that their officers are supposed to be the best in the Italian armed forces, they are not famed for their shining intellectual prowess. As a result, they are the butt of many Italian jokes. For example, in the middle of a lively conversation on a train, someone asked, 'By the way, have you heard the latest joke about the *carabinieri*?' A gentleman sitting opposite visibly stiffened, saying, 'Before you continue, I should perhaps point out that I am a retired General of the *Carabinieri*.' 'Don't worry, sir, we'll explain it to you later.'

> **There is a different police force for every occasion in Italy.**

The law

Italy's legal traditions are impressive and the country has a vast array of wonderful laws to prevent any kind of injustice, inequality or corruption. On paper the Italian legal system, with its written civil and penal codes, seems more or less perfect.

The problems start with law enforcement. Italy's laws would indeed be perfect but for the Italians – who pay little attention to most of them. For example, although seatbelts are compulsory, not all drivers actually wear them (especially in the South where for a time their introduction led to a roaring trade in T-shirts with seatbelts printed on them). The use of car horns is officially prohibited in built-up

> **❝ Italy's laws would indeed be perfect but for the Italians – who pay little attention to most of them. ❞**

areas, where the maximum speed limit is 30 miles per hour, but these regulations are by and large completely ignored by both the public and the police, although the police will enforce them occasionally, especially when they see people driving cars with foreign or out-of-town number plates.

Because of the very serious difficulties the Italian government has in collecting taxes, a whole series of laws exists to make sure regulations are respected. For example, until not long ago receipts issued by bars and restaurants as proof of payment had to be carried a minimum of 50 metres before being thrown away.

Language

Until the end of the Second World War Italian was not widely spoken. It was essentially a written language, mainly used by administrators, bureaucrats, a small caste of academics and the then members of the ruling class. The rest of Italy spoke in their local dialects. It was the advent of television that was the prime force in spreading Italian as it is currently known. These days most Italians understand it, and all young Italians speak it.

> **" Until the end of the Second World War Italian was not widely spoken. "**

One of the many beauties of the language is the ease with which dimension, value or meaning can be altered by simply changing the ending of nouns and adjectives. Thus, a shoe (*scarpa*) can become a skiing/hiking boot (*scarpone*) or Cinderella's slipper (*scarpina*); and doing a *scarpetta* ('making a little shoe') means cleaning one's plate with a bit of bread.

A love (*amore*) can become a sweetheart (*amoroso*), or a cupid (*amorino*), or a mistress (*amante*). Italian men who hear of a *bella donna*, a beautiful woman, will wonder if she is in fact *bellissima* (stunning) or just *bellina* (quite pretty); maybe she is a *bellona* (well past her prime, but still a poser) or perhaps she is *belloccia* (passable, in all senses of the word). And is she worth very little (*donnetta*) or will she charge a fee (*donnac-*

cia)? The only way for the Latin lover to find out is by having a go, unless he is a *donnicciola* – one who is too timorous to try.

Italian has bequeathed to the world a vast number of musical terms: *pianoforte, sonata, aria, primadonna, concerto, adagio, pizzicato, pianissimo, soprano, maestro, virtuoso* and *castrato*. And restaurants worldwide offer *pasta, pizza, mozzarella, zabaglione, grissini, cappuccino, amaretto* and *sambuca*.

For their part, the Italians have adopted and adapted English/American words with huge enthusiasm – *lifting* (face-lift), *telemarketing, cliccare sul mouse* (to click on the mouse), *lo zapping* (channel hopping). They also use English words that English-speakers would hardly recognise: for example, Italian football stars invariably refer to their trainers as '*il Mister*'. English words are even invented and then exported, sometimes with surprising success, such as '*body*', which threatens to replace leotard.

> **The local dialects or languages can be almost impossible for Italians in other regions to understand.**

Dialects

When they are at home in their villages Italians speak the local dialects or languages, which can be almost impossible for *gli altri* in other regions to understand.

One survey found that of the EU's 28 minority language communities, 13 were in Italy. There are French-speaking Italians in the Aosta Valley, German-speaking Italians in the Alto Adige, Slovene- and Serbo-Croat-speaking Italians in Trieste, and Albanian- and Greek-speaking Italians in Puglia, while in Sardinia there are Catalan-speaking Italians. However, with the influx of immigrants, the language map of Italy is changing. The census form is accompanied by 'How to fill it in' instructions in multiple languages, including Arabic and Russian.

❝ There are still a good many Italians who speak a local dialect, and a number of Italians who have no language other than their dialect. ❞

In addition, local dialect is both structurally and lexically very different from Italian. There are still a good many Italians who speak a dialect, and a number of Italians who have no language other than their dialect. It is possible therefore to believe the following tale. A man from the southern region of Puglia, who has lived in the northern region of Piedmont for 20 years, has a Piedmontese neighbour who greets him every day as he leaves for work. The Pugliese man speaks Italian, and the Piedmontese man understands him. But, because the Piedmontese man prefers not to speak Italian and the Pugliese would rather not learn Piedmontese, their conversation remains forever somewhat lop-sided.

The Author

Brought up in England, Martin Solly first became enamoured of Italy as a student, staying with his *amici* in a superb farmhouse complete with swimming pool. The red-earthed landscapes of Tuscany, Renaissance culture, Chianti and mouth-watering *tortellini* and *zucchini* convinced him that the Italians enjoyed the ultimate in sybaritic living.

After working on farms, and in bars, restaurants, bookstores and schools, he settled in Piedmont with the intention of improving his knowledge of things Italian. He little realised this would include a local girl and, ignoring the old Italian saying *Moglie e buoi dei paesi tuoi* ('Choose your wife and your cattle from your own backyard'), he married her and stayed.

Still happily ensconced in the area and the author of numerous books on linguistics and the English language, Solly has never lost the habit of looking around for the queue. He does, however, admit to a distinct penchant for the Alfa-Romeo, and to only ever wearing Italian ties.

The Greeks

Greeks exhibit an extreme passion for freedom of choice – which has turned law circumvention into an art and has made them incapable of comprehending words like 'discipline', 'co-ordination' or 'system'.

The Spanish

Anyone attempting to understand the Spanish must first of all recognise the fact that they do not consider anything important except total enjoyment. If it is not enjoyable it will be ignored.

The Icelanders

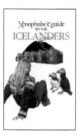

The landscape is so awesome that human beings cannot help but feel insignificant in relation to it. Brought up on tales of a world peopled with curious gods and superheroes, it is understandable that the Icelanders saw the land as the home of supernatural beings.

The English

The English have no talent for handling passion. When confronted by it in others, they will mostly duck down behind their newspapers in embarrassment, and pretend that it isn't happening.

The French

A French man or woman will hold up a piece of nifty reasoning with the same pride that another might feel when displaying an Impressionist painting, a Fabergé egg or a Sèvres vase.

The Americans

Americans are friendly because they just can't help it. But a wise traveller realises that a few happy moments with an American do not translate into a permanent commitment of any kind. This is a nation whose most fundamental social relationship is the casual acquaintance.

On the series:

'If I were a cabaret artist or stand up comedian, I'd just get up and read these books to the audience as they would bring the house down.'   Reviewer of *Het Parool*, Holland

The Americans:

'Very funny, very accurate. Quick bits of information about American habits and attitudes. It had me rolling on the floor, not wanting to admit how much of it is dead on.'   Reader from Georgia, USA

The Swiss:

'This book is Great! I really enjoyed it and found it to be a very thorough reference to the Swiss without being too long and drawn out. It kept me laughing but well informed all the way through. I liked the book so much I want to send a copy to my whole family.'   Reader from Switzerland

The Germans:

'You *must* read this book if you want to learn more about the strange nature of the Germans because you will find most of it in no other book.'   Reader from Stuttgart

Xenophobe's®
guides

Available as printed books and e-books:

The Albanians	The Israelis
The Americans	The Italians
The Aussies	The Japanese
The Austrians	The Kiwis
The Belgians	The Norwegians
The Brazilians	The Poles
The Canadians	The Portuguese
The Chinese	The Russians
The Czechs	The Scots
The Danes	The Spanish
The Dutch	The Swedes
The English	The Swiss
The Estonians	The Welsh
The Finns	
The French	
The Frisians	
The Germans	French
The Greeks	German
The Icelanders	Greek
The Irish	Spanish

Xenophobe's®
lingo learners

Xenophobe's Guides

Xenophobe's® Guides e-books are available from Amazon, iBookstore, and other online sources, and via:

www.xenophobes.com

Xenophobe's® Guides print versions can be purchased through online retailers (Amazon, etc.) or via our web site:

www.xenophobes.com

Xenophobe's® Guides are pleased to offer a quantity discount on book orders. Why not embellish an occasion – a wedding goody bag, a conference or other corporate event with our guides. Or treat yourself to a full set of the paperback edition. Ask us for details:

Xenophobe's® Guides
e-mail: info@xenophobes.com

Xenophobe's® Guides enhance your understanding of the people of different nations. Don't miss out – order your next Xenophobe's® Guide soon.

Xenophobe's Guides